DEFLATION AND LIBERTY

JÖRG GUIDO HÜLSMANN

Ludwig
von Mises
Institute
AUBURN, ALABAMA

Ludwig von Mises Institute
518 West Magnolia Avenue
Auburn, Alabama 36832 U.S.A.
www.mises.org

ISBN: 978-1-933550-35-0

PREFACE

IT IS MY GREAT pleasure to see this little essay in print. Written and presented more than five years ago, it was welcomed at the time by scholars with a background in Austrian economics. However, it was not understood and was rejected by those who did not have this background. In order to reach a broader audience, a short essay would simply not do. I therefore decided not to publish "Deflation and Liberty" and started to work on *The Ethics of Money Production*, a book-length presentation of the argument, which has just become available from the Mises Institute.

In the present crisis, the citizens of the United States have to make an important choice. They can support a policy designed to perpetuate our current fiat money system and the sorry state of banking and of financial markets that it logically entails. *Or* they can support a policy designed to reintroduce a free market in money and finance. This latter policy requires the government to keep its hands off. It should not produce money, nor should it appoint a special agency to produce money. It should not force the citizens to use fiat money by imposing legal tender laws. It should not regulate banking and should not regulate the financial markets. It should not try to fix the interest rate, the prices of financial titles, or commodity prices.

Clearly, these measures are radical by present-day standards, and they are not likely to find sufficient support. But they lack support out of ignorance and fear.

We are told by virtually all the experts on money and finance—the central bankers and most university professors—that the crisis hits us despite the best efforts of the Fed; that money, banking, and financial markets are not meant to be free, because they end up in disarray despite the massive presence of the government as a financial agent, as a regulator, and as money producer; that our monetary system provides us with great benefits that we would be foolish not to preserve. Those same experts therefore urge us to give the government an *even greater* presence in the financial markets, to *increase* its regulatory powers, and to encourage *even more* money production to be used for bailouts.

However, all of these contentions are wrong, as economists have demonstrated again and again since the times of Adam Smith and David Ricardo. A paper money system is not beneficial from an overall point of view. It does not create real resources on which our welfare depends. It merely distributes the existing resources in a different manner; some people gain, others lose. It is a system that makes banks and financial markets vulnerable, because it induces them to economize on the essential safety valves of business: cash and equity. Why hold any substantial cash balances if the central bank stands ready to lend you any amount that might be needed, at a moment's notice? Why use your own money if you can finance your investments with cheap credit from the printing press?

To raise these questions is to answer them. The crisis did not hit us *despite* the presence of our monetary and financial authorities. It hit us *because* of them.

Then there is the fear factor. If we follow a hands-off policy, the majority of experts tell us, the banking industry, the financial markets, and much of the rest of the economy will be wiped out in a bottomless deflationary spiral.

The present essay argues that this is a half-truth. It is true that without further government intervention there would be a deflationary spiral. It is *not* true that this spiral would be bottomless and wipe out the economy. It would *not* be a mortal threat to the lives and the welfare of the general population. It destroys essentially those companies and industries that live a parasitical existence at the expense of the rest of the economy, and which owe their existence to our present fiat money system. Even in the short run, therefore, deflation reduces our real incomes only within rather narrow limits. And it will clear the ground for very substantial growth rates in the medium and long run.

We should not be afraid of deflation. We should love it as much as our liberties.

JÖRG GUIDO HÜLSMANN
Angers, France
October 2008

I.

THE TWENTIETH CENTURY HAS been the century of omnipotent government. In some countries, totalitarian governments have established themselves in one stroke through revolutions—apparently a bad strategy, for none of these governments exists any more. But in other countries, totalitarianism has not sprung into life full-fledged like Venus from the waves. In the United States and in virtually all the western European countries, government has grown slowly but steadily, and if unchecked this growth will make it totalitarian one day, even though this day seems to be far removed from our present.

Fact is that in all western countries the growth of government has been faster over the last one hundred years than the growth of the economy. Its most conspicuous manifestations are the welfare state and of the warfare state.[1] Now the growth of the welfare-warfare state would not have been possible without inflation,

---

[1]In the American case, the warfare state has been a more powerful engine of government growth than the welfare state; see Robert Higgs, *Crisis and Leviathan: Critical Episodes in the Growth of American Government* (New York: Oxford University Press, 1987).

which for the purposes of our study we can define as
the growth of the supply of base money and of financial titles that are redeemable into base money on
demand.[2] The production of ever-new quantities of
paper dollars and the creation of ever-new credit facil-
ities at the Federal Reserve have provided the "liquidity" for an even greater expansion of bank-created
demand deposits and other money substitutes, which
in turn allowed for an unparalleled expansion of public debt. U.S. public debt is currently (December 2002)
at some 6.2 trillion dollars, up from under 2 trillion at
the beginning of the 1980s, and less than 1 trillion
before the era of the paper dollar set in when Presi-
dent Nixon closed the gold window in the early 1970s.

The link between the paper dollar and the expo-
nential expansion of public debt is well known. From
the point of view of the creditors, the federal government controls the Federal Reserve—the monopoly producer of paper dollars—and it can therefore never go
bankrupt. If necessary, the federal government can
have any quantity of dollars printed to pay back its

---

[2]With this definition we follow Murray N. Rothbard, *Man, Economy,
and State,* 3rd ed. (Auburn, Ala.: Ludwig von Mises Institute), p. 851,
who defines inflation as an increase of the quantity of money greater
than an increase in specie. While Rothbard's definition fits the case of
a fractional-reserve banking system based on a commodity money
standard, our definition is meant to fit the specific case of a fiat money
standard with fractional-reserve banking. Both definitions deviate from
the most widespread connotation of the term, according to which
inflation is an increase of the money price level. The latter definition
is not very useful for our purposes, because we intend to analyze the
causal impact of changes in the supply of base money (which is at all
times subject to political control).

debt. Buying government bonds is thus backed up with a security that no other debtor can offer. And the federal government can constantly expand its activities and finance them through additional debt even if there is no prospect at all that these debts will ever be paid back out of tax revenues. The result is seemingly unchecked growth of those governments that control the production of paper money.

Among the many causes that coincided in bringing about this state of affairs is a certain lack of resistance on the part of professional economists. In the present essay I will deal with a wrong idea that has prevented many economists and other intellectuals from fighting inflation with the necessary determination. Most economists backed off from opposing inflation precisely when it was needed most, namely, at the few junctures of history when the inflationary system was about to collapse. Rather than impartially analyzing the event, they started fearing deflation more than inflation, and thus ended up supporting "reflation"—which in fact is nothing but *further* inflation.[3]

---

[3]For the purposes of our study we will define deflation as a reduction of the quantity of base money, or of financial titles that are redeemable into base money on demand. Again, this deviates from the usual connotation of the term, which defines deflation as a decrease of the price level. But as the reader will see, our analysis will cover both phenomena—deflation in our definition and a decrease of the price level. The point of our definition is merely to render our analysis more suitable for practical application. A monetary authority at all times can prevent deflation in our definition, while it can at times be unable to prevent a decrease of the price level, even by pumping great quantities of base money into the economy.

The United States of America has experienced two
such junctures: the years of the Great Depression and
the little depression we are facing right now in the
wake of the first global stock market boom. Today
again, the deflationary collapse of our monetary system is a very real possibility. In November 2002, offi-
cials of the Federal Reserve (Greenspan, Bernanke)
and of the Bank of England (Bean) proclaimed there
would be no limit to the amount of money they would
print to fend off deflation. These plans reflect what
today is widely regarded as orthodoxy in monetary
matters. Even many critics of the inflationary policies
of the past concede that, under present circumstances,
some inflation might be beneficial, if it is used to combat deflation. Some of them point out that there is *not
yet* any deflation, and that therefore there is no need
to intensify the use of the printing press. But on the
other hand they agree in principle that *if* a major deflation set in, there would be a political need for more
spending, and that, to finance the increased spending,
the governments should incur more debts and that the
central banks should print more money.[4]

Such views have a certain prominence even among
Austrian economists. Ludwig von Mises, Hans
Sennholz, Murray Rothbard, and other Austrians are

---

[4]See for example the columns and editorials by journalists with a
hard-money reputation such as Steve Forbes in the U.S. and Stefan
Baron in Germany. The same message emanates from the publica-
tions of otherwise reasonable economists such as Jude Wanniski and
Norbert Walter. A symptomatic essay is Norbert Walter, "Is the Global
Recession Over?" *Internationale Politik* (Transatlantic Edition, fall
2002): 85–89.

known for their intransigent opposition to inflation. But only Sennholz did not flinch from *praising deflation* and depression when it came to abolishing fiat money and putting a sound money system in its place. By contrast, Mises and Rothbard championed deflation only to the extent it accelerated the readjustment of the economy in a bust that followed a period of inflationary boom. But they explicitly (Mises) and implicitly (Rothbard) sought to avoid deflation in all other contexts. In particular, when it came to monetary reform, both Mises and Rothbard championed schemes to "redefine" a paper currency's "price of gold" to restore convertibility.[5]

---

[5]See Hans Sennholz, *The Age of Inflation* (1979), chap. 6; Rothbard, *Man, Economy, and State*, pp. 863–66; idem, *America's Great Depression*, 5th ed. (Auburn, Ala.: Ludwig von Mises Institute, 1999), pp. 14–19; Ludwig von Mises, "Die geldtheoretische Seite des Stabilisierungsproblems," *Schriften des Vereins für Sozialpolitik* 164, no. 2 (1923); idem, *Theory of Money and Credit* (Indianapolis: Liberty Fund, 1980), pp. 262–68, 453–500; idem, *Human Action*, Scholar's Edition (Auburn, Ala.: Ludwig von Mises Institute, 1998), pp. 564f.; Murray N. Rothbard, *The Mystery of Banking* (New York: Richardson and Snyder, 1983), pp. 263–69; idem, *The Case Against the Fed* (Auburn, Ala.: Ludwig von Mises Institute, 1995), pp. 145–51. Mises and Rothbard adopted the point of view espoused already by Jean-Baptiste Say, who depicted deflation as a harmful practice of restoring monetary sanity after a period of extended inflation. See Jean-Baptiste Say, *Traité d'économie politique*, 6th ed. (Paris, 1841); translated as *A Treatise on Political Economy* (Philadelphia: Claxton, Rensen & Haffelfinger, 1880). For a critical survey of the opinions of Austrian economists on deflation, see Philipp Bagus, "Deflation: When Austrians Become Interventionists" (working paper, Auburn, Ala.: Ludwig von Mises Institute, April 2003).

The main weakness of this scheme is that it implies that the reform process be directed by the very institutions and persons whom the reform is supposed to make more or less superfluous. It is also questionable whether our monetary authorities can legitimately use "their" gold reserves to salvage their paper money. In fact, they have come to control these reserves through a confiscatory coup, and it is therefore not at all clear how plans for monetary reform à la Mises and Rothbard can be squared with the libertarian legal or moral principles that Rothbard champions in other works.

But there is also another issue that needs to be addressed: what is actually wrong with deflating the money supply, from an economic point of view? This question will be at center stage here, which can fortunately build on Rothbard's analysis of deflation, which demonstrated in particular the beneficial role that deflation can have in speeding up the readjustment of the productive structure after a financial crisis. But no economist seems to have been interested in further pursuing the sober analysis of the impact of deflation on the market process, and of its social and political consequences. The truth is that deflation has become the scapegoat of the economics profession. It is not analyzed, but derided. One hundred years of pro-inflation propaganda have created a quasi-total agreement on the issue.[6] Wherever we turn, deflation is uniformly

---

[6]The main engines of the propaganda have been the state universities of the West, as well as an exaggerated faith in the authority of monetary "experts" in the service of the IMF, the World Bank, the Federal Reserve, and other government agencies charged with the technical details of spreading inflation. Is it really necessary to point out the *non sequitur* implied in granting expert status in matters monetary to the

presented in bad terms, and each writer hurries to present the fight against deflation as the bare minimum of economic statesmanship. Economists who otherwise cannot agree on any subject are happy to find common ground in the heart-felt condemnation of deflation. In their eyes, the case against deflation is so clear that they do not even bother about it. The libraries of our universities contain hundreds of books splitting hairs about unemployment, business cycles, and so on. But they rarely feature a monograph on deflation. Its evilness is beyond dispute.[7]

---

employees of these organizations? An obvious parallel is the case of the economists on the payroll of labor unions who, because "labor" unions pay them, are considered to be experts in labor economics. Clearly, if one called labor unions "associations for the destruction of the labor market"—which most of them are by any objective standard—the expertise of their employees would stand in a more sober light. The same thing holds true for those writers on monetary affairs who happen to be on the payroll of the various associations for the destruction of our money. This is of course not to deny that there might be good economists working for the IMF or the Federal Reserve. Our point is merely that their qualification to speak on the issue is not at all enhanced by their professional affiliation. Quite to the contrary, given the incentive structure, we would have to expect that good monetary economists only accidentally find their way to these institutions.

[7]The outstanding modern theoretician of deflation is Murray N. Rothbard. As we have stated above, Rothbard's views on deflation seem to be deficient only when it comes to the practical issue of monetary reform. An overview of the essential tenets of Austrian deflation theory is in Joseph T. Salerno, "An Austrian Taxonomy of Deflation" (working paper, Auburn, Ala.: Ludwig von Mises Institute, February 2002). Among the few non-Austrian works that analyze deflation without undue emotional bias, see John Wheatley, *An Essay on the Theory of Money and Principles of Commerce* (London: Bulmer & Co., 1807), in particular Wheatley's discussion of Lord Grenville's plan for monetary reform on pp. 346–57; Lancelot Hare, *Currency and Employment,*

Yet this silent accord stands on shaky ground. A frank and enthusiastic *endorsement of deflation* is, at any rate in our time, one of the most important requirements to safeguard the future of liberty.

II.

WHEN IT COMES TO matters of money and banking, all practical political issues ultimately hinge on one central question: Can one improve or deteriorate the state of an economy by increasing or decreasing the quantity of money?[8]

Aristotle said that money was no part of the wealth of a nation because it was simply a medium of exchange in inter-regional trade, and the authority of his opinion thoroughly marked medieval thought on money. Scholastic scholars therefore spent no time enquiring about the benefits that changes of the money supply could have for the economy. The relevant issue in their eyes was the legitimacy of debasements, because they saw that this was an important

---

Deflation of the Currency—A Reply to the Anti-Deflationists (London: P.S. King & Son, 1921); Edwin Cannan, *The Paper Pound of 1797–1821,* 2nd ed. (London: King & Son, 1925); Yves Guyot, *Les problèmes de la deflation* (Paris: Félix Alcan, 1923); Guyot, Yves and Arthur Raffalovich, *Inflation et déflation* (Paris: Félix Alcan, 1923).

[8]Speaking of "an economy" we mean the group of persons using the same money. Our analysis therefore concerns both open and closed economies in the usual connotations of the terms, which relates closedness and openness to political borders separating different groups of persons.

issue of distributive justice.⁹ And after the birth of economic science in the eighteenth century, the classical
economists too did not deny this essential point. David
Hume, Adam Smith, and Étienne de Condillac
observed that money is neither a consumers' good nor
a producers' good and that, therefore, its quantity is
irrelevant for the wealth of a nation.¹⁰ This crucial
insight would also inspire the intellectual battles of the
next four or five generations of economists—men such
as Jean-Baptiste Say, David Ricardo, John Stuart Mill,
Frédéric Bastiat, and Carl Menger—who constantly
made the case for sound money.

As a result, the western world had much more
sound money in the nineteenth century than in the
twentieth century. Large strata of the population paid
and were paid in coins made out of precious metals,
especially out of gold and silver. It was money that
made these citizens, however humble their social status, sovereign in monetary affairs. The art of coinage
flourished and produced coins that could be authenti-
cated by every market participant.

---

⁹See Aristotle, *Politics*, book 2, chap. 9; *Nicomachian Ethics*, book V,
in particular chap. 11; Nicolas Oresme, "Traité sur l'origine, la nature,
le droit et les mutations des monnaies," *Traité des monnaies et autres
écrits monétaires du XIV siècle*, Claude Dupuy, ed. (Lyon: La
Manufacture, 1989); Juan de Mariana, "A Treatise on the Alteration of
Money," *Markets and Morality* 5, no. 2 ([1609] 2002).

¹⁰See David Hume, "On Money," *Essays* (Indianapolis: Liberty Fund,
[1752] 1985), p. 288; Adam Smith, *Wealth of Nations* (New York:
Random House, [1776] 1994), book 2, chap. 2, in part. pp. 316f.;
Condillac, *Le commerce et le gouvernement*. 2nd ed. (Paris: Letellier &
Mradan, 1795), in part. p. 86; translated as *Commerce and
Government* (Cheltenham, U.K.: Elgar, 1997).

Some present-day libertarians harbor a romantic picture of these days of the "classical gold standard." And it is true that it was the golden age of monetary institutions in the West, especially when we compare them with our own time, in which the monetary equivalent of Alchemy has risen to the status of orthodoxy. But it is also true that western monetary institutions in the era of the classical gold standard were far from being perfect. Governments still enjoyed monopoly power in the field of coinage, a remnant of the medieval "regalia" privileges that prevented the discovery of better coins and coin systems through entrepreneurial competition. Governments frequently intervened in the production of money through price control schemes, which they camouflaged with the pompous name of "bimetallism." They actively promoted fractional-reserve banking, which promised ever-new funds for the public treasury. And they promoted the emergence of central banking through special monopoly charters for a few privileged banks. The overall result of these laws was to facilitate the introduction of inflationary paper currencies and to drive specie out of circulation. At the beginning of the nineteenth century, most of Europe, insofar as it knew monetary exchange at all, used paper currencies.[11] And during the

---

[11]At the time John Wheatley observed:

> In England, Scotland, and Ireland, in Denmark, and in Austria, scarcely any thing but paper is visible. In Spain, Portugal, Prussia, Sweden, and European Russia, paper has a decisive superiority. And in France, Italy, and Turkey only, the prevalence of specie is apparent. (*An Essay on the Theory of Money and Principles of Commerce*, p. 287)

remainder of that century, things did not change much. England alone among the major nations was on the gold standard during the greater part of the nineteenth century, and banknotes of the Bank of England played a much greater role in monetary exchanges than specie—in fact, the reserve ratio of the Bank seems to have been around 3 percent for most of the time, and occasionally it was even lower.[12]

In short, the monetary constitutions of the nineteenth century were not perfect, and neither would the monetary thought of the classical economists satisfy us today.[13] David Hume believed that inflation could stimulate production in the short run. Adam Smith believed that inflation in the form of credit expansion was beneficial if it was "backed up" with a "corresponding amount" of real goods, and Jean-Baptiste Say similarly endorsed expansions of the quantity of money that accommodated the "needs of commerce." Smith and

---

[12]See Jacob Viner, "International Aspects of the Gold Standard," *Gold and Monetary Stabilization*, Quincy Wright, ed. (Chicago, Chicago University Press, 1932), pp. 5, 12. Viner emphasizes that the pre-World War I gold standard was not fundamentally different from the interwar gold-exchange standard. It "was a managed standard" (p. 17). This attenuates the thesis of Jacques Rueff that the gold-exchange standard introduced something like a quantum-leap deterioration into the international monetary system. See Rueff, *The Monetary Sin of the West* (New York: Macmillan, 1972).

[13]For a recent essay criticizing some of the main fallacies of classical monetary thought, see Nikolay Gertchev, "The Case For Gold—Review Essay," *Quarterly Journal of Austrian Economics* 6, no. 4 (2003).

Ricardo suggested increasing the wealth of the nation by substituting inherently value-less paper tickets for metallic money. John Stuart Mill championed the notion that sound money means money of stable value. These errors in the monetary thought of Hume, Smith, Ricardo, and Mill were of course almost negligible in comparison to their central insight, to repeat, that the wealth of a nation does not depend on changes in the quantity of money. But eventually a new generation of students, infected with the virus of statism—worship of the state—brushed over that central insight, and thus the *errors* of the classical economists, rather than their science, triumphed in the twentieth century.

Men such as Irving Fisher, Knut Wicksell, Karl Helfferich, Friedrich Bendixen, Gustav Cassel, and especially John Maynard Keynes set out on a relentless campaign against the gold standard. These champions of inflation conceded the insight of the classical economists, that the wealth of a nation did not depend on its money supply, but they argued that this was true only in the long run. In the short run, the printing press could work wonders. It could reduce unemployment and stimulate production and economic growth.

Who could reject such a horn of plenty? And why? Most economists point out the costs of inflation in terms of loss of purchasing power—estimates run as high as a 98 percent reduction of the U.S. dollar's purchasing power since the Federal Reserve took control of the money supply. What is less well known are the concomitant effects of the century-long great dollar inflation. Paper money has produced several great crises, each of which turned out to be more severe than the preceding one. Moreover, paper money has completely transformed the financial structure of the western economies. At the beginning of the twentieth century, most firms and industrial corporations were financed out of their revenues, and banks and other financial intermediaries played only a subordinate role. Today, the picture has been reversed, and the most fundamental reason for this reversal is paper money. Paper money has caused an unprecedented increase of debt on all levels: government, corporate, and individual. It has financed the growth of the state on all levels, federal, state, and local. It thus has become the technical foundation for the totalitarian menace of our days.

In the light of these long-term consequences of inflation, its alleged short-run benefits lose much of their attractiveness. But the great irony is that even these short-run benefits in terms of employment and growth are illusory. Sober reflection shows that there are no systematic short-run benefits of inflation at all. In other words, whatever benefits might result from inflation are largely the accidental result of inflation hitting a particularly favorable set of circumstances, and we have no reason to assume that these accidental benefits are more likely to occur than accidental harm—quite to the contrary! The main impact of inflation is to bring about a redistribution of resources. There are therefore short-run benefits for certain members of society, but these benefits balanced by short-run losses for other citizens.

The great French economist Frédéric Bastiat made the quite general point that the visible blessings that result from government intervention into the market economy are in fact only one set of consequences that

follow from this intervention. But there is another set
of consequences that the government does not like to
talk about because they demonstrate the futility of the
intervention. When the government taxes its citizens to
give subsidies to a steel producer, the benefits to the
steel firm, its employees, and stockholders are patent.
But other interests have suffered from the intervention.
In particular, the taxpayers have less money to patron-
ize other businesses. And these other businesses and
their customers are also harmed by the policy because
the steel firm is now able to pay higher wages and
higher rents, thus bidding away the factors of production that are also needed in other branches of industry.

And so it is with inflation. There is absolutely no reason why an increase in the quantity of money should
create more rather than less growth. It is true that the
firms who receive money fresh from the printing press
are thereby benefited. But other firms are harmed by
the very same fact because they can no longer pay the
higher prices for wages and rents that the privileged
firm can now pay. And all other owners of money,
whether they are entrepreneurs or workers, are
harmed too, because their money now has a lower
purchasing power than it would otherwise have had.

Similarly, there is no reason why inflation should
ever reduce rather than increase unemployment. People
become unemployed or remain unemployed when they
do not wish to work, or if they are forcibly prevented
from working for the wage rate an employer is willing
to pay. Inflation does not change this fact. What inflation does is to reduce the purchasing power of each
money unit. If the workers anticipate these effects, they
will ask for higher nominal wages as a compensation for

the loss of purchasing power. In this case, inflation has no effect on unemployment. Quite to the contrary, it can even have negative effects, namely, if the workers *over*estimate the inflation-induced reduction of their real wages and thus ask for wage-rate increases that bring about even more unemployment. Only if they do not know that the quantity of money has been increased to lure them into business at current wage rates will they consent to work rather than remaining unemployed. All plans to reduce unemployment through inflation therefore boil down to fooling the workers—a childish strategy, to say the least.[14]

For the same reason, inflation is no remedy for the problem of "sticky wages"—that is, for the problem of coercive labor unions. Wages are sticky only to the extent that the workers choose not to work. But the crucial question is: How long can they afford not to work? And the answer to this question is that this period is constrained within the very narrow limits of their savings. As soon as a worker's personal savings are exhausted, he willy-nilly starts offering his services even at lower wage rates. It follows that in a free labor

---

[14]See in particular Mises, *Die Ursachen der Wirtschaftskrise* (Tübingen: Mohr, 1931); translated as "The Causes of the Economic Crisis," in *On the Manipulation of Money and Credit* (Dobbs Ferry, N.Y.: Free Market Books, 1978). See also Mises, "Wages, Unemployment, and Inflation," *Christian Economics* 4 (March 1958); reprinted in Mises, *Planning For Freedom,* 4th ed. (South Holland, Ill.: Libertarian Press, 1974), pp. 150ff. The long-standing presence of mass unemployment in Germany, France, and other European countries seems to be a smashing refutation of the Keynesian hypothesis. If anything, the labor unions in these countries clearly seem to overestimate the inflation rate.

market, wages *are* sufficiently flexible at any point of time. Stickiness comes into play only as a result of government intervention, in particular in the form of (a) tax-financed unemployment relief and of (b) legislation giving the labor unions a monopoly of the labor supply.

Since we are not concerned here with questions of labor economics, we can directly turn to the connection between employment and monetary policy. Does inflation solve the problem of sticky wages? The answer is in the negative, and for the same reasons we pointed out above. Inflation can overcome the problem of sticky wages only to the extent that the paper money producers can surprise the labor unions. To the extent that the latter anticipate the moves of the masters of the printing press, inflation will either not reduce unemployment at all, or even increase it further.[15]

III.

FROM THE STANDPOINT OF the commonly shared interests of all members of society, the quantity of money is irrelevant. Any quantity of money provides all the services that indirect exchange can possibly provide, both in the long run *and* in the short run. This fact is the

---

[15]On the entire issue see in particular William Harold Hutt, *The Theory of Collective Bargaining* (San Francisco: Cato Institute, [1954] 1980); idem, The *Strike-Threat System* (New Rochelle, N.Y.: Arlington House, 1973); idem, *The Keynesian Episode* (Indianapolis: Liberty Press, 1979).

unshakable starting point for any sound reflection on monetary matters.

And it is the most important criterion when it comes to dealing with deflation. In light of the principle discovered by the classical economists, we can say that deflation is certainly not what it is commonly alleged to be: a curse for all members of society. Deflation is a monetary phenomenon, and as such *it does* affect the distribution of wealth among the individuals and various strata of society, as well as the relative importance of the different branches of industry. But it does *not* affect the aggregate wealth of society. Deflation is a drastic reduction of the quantity of money or of money substitutes, and it entails a precipitous decline of money prices. Such an event, be it ever so dramatic for a great number of individuals, is most certainly not a mortal threat for society as a whole.[16]

Imagine if all prices were to drop tomorrow by 50 percent. Would this affect our ability to feed, cloth, shelter, and transport ourselves? It would not, because the disappearance of money is not paralleled by a disappearance of the physical structure of production. In

---

[16]This is also recognized, implicitly at least, in the few works of management literature that deal with entrepreneurship in a deflationary environment. See for example Daniel Stelter, *Deflationäre Depression: Konsequenzen für das Management* (Wiesbaden: Deutscher Universitäts-Verlag, 1991); A.G. Shilling, *Deflation: Why It's Coming, Whether It's Good or Bad, and How It Will Affect Your Investments, Business, and Personal Affairs* (Short Hill, N.J.: Lakeview, 1998); idem, *Deflation: How to Survive and Thrive in the Coming Wave of Deflation* (New York: McGraw-Hill, 1999); Robert R. Prechter, *Conquer the Crash: You Can Survive and Prosper in a Deflationary Depression* (New York: Wiley, 2002).

a very dramatic deflation, there is much less money around than there used to be, and thus we cannot sell our products and services at the same money prices as before. But our tools, our machines, the streets, the cars and trucks, our crops and our food supplies—all this is still in place. And thus we can go on producing, and even producing profitably, because profit does not depend on the level of money prices at which we sell, but on the difference between the prices at which we sell and the prices at which we buy. In a deflation, both sets of prices drop, and as a consequence for-profit production can go on.

There is only one fundamental change that deflation brings about. It radically modifies the structure of ownership. Firms financed per credits go bankrupt because at the lower level of prices they can no longer pay back the credits they had incurred without anticipating the deflation. Private households with mortgages and other considerable debts to pay back go bankrupt, because with the decline of money prices their monetary income declines too whereas their debts remain at the nominal level. The very attempt to liquidate assets to pay back debt entails a further reduction of the value of those assets, thus making it even more difficult for them to come even with their creditors. In the memorable words of Irving Fisher: "The more the debtors pay, the more they owe."

Yet from this correct observation, Fisher jumped to the fallacious statement that "the liquidation defeats itself."[17] Let us emphasize again that bankruptcies—irre-

---

[17]Irving Fisher, "The Debt-Deflation Theory of Great Depressions," *Econometrica* 1, no. 4 (October 1933): 344. See also Lionel D. Edie,

spective of how many individuals are involved—do not affect the real wealth of the nation, and in particular that they do not prevent the successful continuation of production. The point is that *other* people will run the firms and own the houses—people who at the time the deflation set in were out of debt and had cash in their hands to buy firms and real estate. These new owners can run the firms profitably at the much lower level of selling prices because they bought the stock, and will buy other factors of production, at lower prices too.

In short, the true crux of deflation is that it does not hide the redistribution going hand in hand with changes in the quantity of money. It entails visible misery for many people, to the benefit of equally visible winners. This starkly contrasts with inflation, which creates anonymous winners at the expense of anonymous losers. Both deflation and inflation are, from the point of view we have so far espoused, zero-sum games. But inflation is a secret rip-off and thus the perfect vehicle for the exploitation of a population through its (false) elites, whereas deflation means open redistribution through bankruptcy according to the law.

"The Future of the Gold Standard," *Gold and Monetary Stabilization*, Quincy Wright, ed. (Chicago: Chicago University Press, 1932), pp. 111–30. On pp. 122–26, Edie calls for the stabilization of what Keynes would later call aggregate demand.

IV.

WITH THESE STATEMENTS WE could close our analysis. We have seen that deflation is not inherently bad, and that it is therefore far from being obvious that a wise monetary policy should seek to prevent it, or dampen its effects, at any price. Deflation creates a great number of losers, and many of these losers are perfectly innocent people who have just not been wise enough to anticipate the event. But deflation *also* creates many winners, and it *also* punishes many "political entrepreneurs" who had thrived on their intimate connections to those who control the production of fiat money.

Deflation is certainly not some sort of a reversal of a previous inflation that repairs the harm done in prior redistributions. It brings about a new round of redistribution that *adds* to the previous round of inflation-induced redistribution.[18] But it would be an error to infer from this fact that a deflation following a foregoing inflation was somehow harmful from an economic point, because it would involve additional redistributions. The point is that *any* monetary policy has redistributive effects. In particular, once a deflation of the supply of money substitutes sets in, the only way to combat this is through inflation of the supply of base money, and this policy too involves redistribution and thus creates winners and losers.

---

[18]See Mises, *Theory of Money and Credit*, pp. 262f.; idem, *Human Action*, p. 414.

It follows that there is no *economic* rationale for monetary policy to take up an ardent fight against deflation, rather than letting deflation run its course. Either policy does not benefit the nation as a whole, but merely benefits a part of the nation at the expense of other groups. No civil servant can loyally serve all of his fellow-citizens through a hard-nosed stance against deflation. And neither can he invoke the authority of economic science to buttress such a policy.

But there is also another point of view that merits consideration and which is in fact decisive for our problem. It results from the fact that, in practice, there are at any point in time two, and only two, fundamental options for monetary policy. The first option is to increase the quantity of paper money. The second option is not to increase the paper money supply. Now the question is how well each of these options harmonizes with the basic principles on which a free society is built.

V.

HOW WOULD MONEY BE produced in a free society? Let us first observe that the fact that the quantity of money is irrelevant for the wealth of a nation must not be confused with the *ideal* of stabilizing the quantity of money. The latter ideal is in fact a spurious ideal and does not follow from the aforementioned fact. There is nothing wrong with increases or decreases of the quantity of money. The point is that such increases or decreases should not be mistaken to benefit society as a whole. Right and wrong in monetary policy does not concern the question: *To which end* should the quantity of money be modified? Rather, it concerns the question: *Who* has the right to modify the quantity of money? And in a free society, the obvious answer is: all producers of money have the right to produce more money, and all owners of money have the right to use their property as they see fit.

In a truly free society, the production of money is a matter of private initiative. Money is produced and sold just as any other commodity or service. And this means in particular that in a free society the production of money is competitive. It is a matter of mining precious metals and of minting coins, and both mining and minting are subject to the competition emanating from all other market participants. In selling his product, the money producer competes with all other people who own money and seek to buy the same goods that he desires. And in buying factors of production, the money producer competes with the producers of chairs, theater performances, telephones, carpets, cars and so on. In a word, in a free society the production of money is constrained within fairly narrow limits, limits that are determined by the willingness of other members of society to cooperate with our money producer rather than with someone else.

What kind of money would prevail in a free society? Theoretical considerations and historical experience all point to the same answer: A free society would use precious metals as money. Payments would be made in coins made out of gold, silver, platinum, copper, or whatever other substance would combine scarcity with the physical advantages of these metals.

By contrast, paper money has always been fiat money, that is, it has always been imposed by the coercive power of the state. It is not the money of the free market, but the money of a partially enslaved society.

VI.

The production of money in a free society is a matter of free association. Everybody from the miners to the owners of the mines, to the minters, and up to the customers who buy the minted coins, all of them benefit from the production of money. None of them violates the property rights of anybody else, because everybody is free to enter the mining and minting business, and nobody is obliged to buy the product.

Things are completely different once we turn to money production in interventionist regimes, which have prevailed in the West for the better part of the past 150 years. Here we need to mention in particular two institutional forms of monetary interventionism: (fraudulent) fractional-reserve banking and fiat money. The common characteristic of both these institutions is that they violate the principle of free association. They enable the producers of paper money and of money titles to expand their production through the violation of other people's property rights.

Banking is fraudulent whenever bankers sell uncovered or only partially covered money substitutes that they present as fully covered titles for money. These bankers sell more money substitutes than they

could have sold if they had taken care to keep a 100
percent reserve for each substitute they issued.[19]

The producer of fiat money (in our days typically:
paper money) sells a product that cannot withstand the
competition of free-market monies such as gold and
silver coins, and which the market participants only
use because the use of all other monies is severely
restricted or even outlawed. The most eloquent illus-
tration of this fact is that paper money in all countries
has been protected through legal tender laws. Paper
money is inherently fiat money; it cannot thrive but
when it is imposed by the state.[20]

In both cases, the production of money is *excessive*
because it is no longer constrained by the informed
and voluntary association of the buying public. On a

---

[19]See Hans-Hermann Hoppe, Jörg Guido Hülsmann, and Walter
Block, "Against Fiduciary Media" *Quarterly Journal of Austrian
Economics* 1, no. 1 (Spring 1998): 19–50; Hülsmann, "Has Fractional-
Reserve Banking Really Passed the Market Test?" *Independent Review*
7, no. 3 (2003); and the literature quoted in Hülsmann, "Banks Cannot
Create Money" *Independent Review* 5, no. 1 (2000). This point is by
the way undisputed by all participants in the present debate on frac-
tional-reserve banking. In contrast to the present author, however,
Lawrence White seems to believe that historical fractional-reserve
banking has rarely if ever been fraudulent. See White, "Accounting For
Fractional-Reserve Banknotes and Deposits—or, What's Twenty Quid
to the Bloody Midland Bank?" *Independent Review* 7, no. 3 (2003).

[20]Notice that this point holds true only for genuine paper monies, not
necessarily for national paper currencies consisting of money substitutes backed by commodity money. Neither does our contention necessarily apply to credit monies, such as the paper pound during the
Napoleonic Wars. For the distinction between money, fiat money, and
credit money, see Mises, *Theory of Money and Credit*, pp. 73–76.

free market, paper money could not sustain the competition of the far superior metal monies. The production of any quantity of paper money is therefore excessive by the standards of a free society. Similarly, fractional-reserve banking produces excessive quantities of money substitutes, at any rate in those cases in which the customers are not informed that they are offered fractional-reserve bank deposits, rather than genuine money titles.

This excessive production of money and money titles is inflation by the Rothbardian definition, which we have adapted in the present study to the case of paper money. Inflation is an unjustifiable redistribution of income in favor of those who receive the new money and money titles first, and to the detriment of those who receive them last. In practice the redistribution always works out in favor of the fiat-money producers themselves (whom we misleadingly call "central banks") and of their partners in the banking sector and at the stock exchange. And of course inflation works out to the advantage of governments and their closest allies in the business world. Inflation is the vehicle through which these individuals and groups enrich themselves, unjustifiably, at the expense of the citizenry at large. If there is any truth to the socialist caricature of capitalism—an economic system that exploits the poor to the benefit of the rich—then this caricature holds true for a capitalist system strangulated by inflation. The relentless influx of paper money makes the wealthy and powerful richer and more powerful than they would be if they depended exclusively on the voluntary support of their fellow citizens. And because it shields the political and economic establishment of the country from the competition emanating from the rest of society, inflation puts a brake on social mobility. The rich stay rich (longer) and the poor stay poor (longer) than they would in a free society.[21]

The famous economist Josef Schumpeter once presented inflation as the harbinger of innovation. As he had it, inflationary issues of banknotes would serve to finance upstart entrepreneurs who had great

---

[21]In this regard, inflation works in an unholy alliance with the tax code. The main advantage of the successful newcomer is that he has high revenues. But present-day corporate and income tax rates effectively prevent him from accumulating capital quickly enough to sustain the competition of the establishment. As a result, there are virtually no more firms that make it from the very bottom into the major league of corporate capitalism. It took a technological revolution to overcome these obstacles and bring a few firms such as Microsoft to the top of corporate America. Most other firms are increasingly dependent on credit to finance any large-scale ventures. But financial intermediation is today a highly regulated business, and all major banks are already allied with the industrial establishment. What would be their incentive to finance a venture that destroys the value of some of their other holdings?

A similar situation prevails in individual finance. Consider just the most important case of private debt, namely, debts incurred for building or purchasing a home. Under the prevailing tax code, individuals can deduct interest they pay on their mortgages from their tax bill, but they cannot make any similar deductions if they finance their home out of their own pocket. The result is that virtually nobody even thinks of financing a home the way it has been done in former times, namely, by first saving money and then paying for the house in cash. And paper money has made it possible to always provide new credits for willing homeowners. The printing press of the Federal Reserve has fueled a housing boom just as it has fueled the 1990s boom of the stock market. The stock market boom has already ended in a resounding crash. The housing boom is next in line.

ideas but lacked capital.[22] Now, even if we abstract
from the questionable ethical character of this pro-
posal, which boils down to subsidizing any self-
appointed innovator at the involuntary expense of all
other members of society, we must say that, in light
of practical experience, Schumpeter's scheme is wish-
ful thinking. Credit expansion financed through printing money is in practice the very opposite of a way
to combat the economic establishment. It is the pre-
ferred means of survival for an establishment that cannot, or can no longer, sustain the competition of its
competitors.

It would not be uncharitable to characterize inflation as a large-scale rip-off, in favor of the politically
well-connected few, and to the detriment of the politically destitute masses. It always goes in hand with the
concentration of political power in the hands of those
who are privileged to own a banking license and of
those who control the production of the monopoly
paper money. It promotes endless debts, puts society
at the mercy of "monetary authorities" such as central
banks, and to that extent entails moral corruption of
society.[23]

---

[22]See Josef A. Schumpeter, *Theorie der wirtschaftlichen Entwicklung*
(Leipzig: Duncker & Humblot, 1911); translated as *Theory of Economic
Development* (Cambridge, Mass.: Harvard University Press, 1949).

[23]See on this point the concise statements in Robert Higgs, "Inflation
and the Destruction of the Free Market Economy," *Intercollegiate
Review* (Spring 1979).

VII.

INFLATION IN THE FORM of fractional-reserve banking and
fiat money is ultimately a self-defeating practice. It
bears in itself the germs of its own destruction and, as
we shall see, deflation is the essential vehicle of this
destruction. We can distinguish three scenarios of the
halt of inflationary processes:[24]

First, there can be a liquidity crisis of the fractional-
reserve banking system that ends up in a bank run,
that is, in a sharp decline of the demand for money
substitutes. The concomitant drastic reduction of the
money supply entails a corresponding decrease of
money prices, which negatively affects all market participants who have financed their operations through
debt. The lower nominal selling receipts after the run
do not suffice to pay back the debts contracted at the

---

[24]See Jörg Guido Hülsmann, "Toward A General Theory of Error
Cycles," *Quarterly Journal of Austrian Economics* 1, no. 4 (1998).
Fractional-reserve banking melts down whenever, and for whatever
reason, a sufficiently big number of bank customers decide to
demand redemption of their deposits. Any increase of the quantity of
money can engender a sequence of boom and bust, if (a) the new
money first reaches the capital markets and if (b) the entrepreneurs
do not anticipate that the new money will lead to a rise in prices over
the level they would otherwise have reached. The erroneous calcula-
tions of the entrepreneurs lead them to shift resources from sustain-
able investment projects into ones that cannot be completed with the
available quantities of factors of production. And the erroneous cal-
culations are also reflected in (not caused by) a below-equilibrium
interest rate. When the market participants discover their errors, the
more or less large number of unsustainable firms goes bankrupt, thus
upsetting the balance sheets of the banks and entailing a financial
meltdown.

higher nominal price level of the past. This in turn jeopardizes the positions of many creditors, who when they do not get their money back cannot pay back *their* creditors. Thus the liquidity crisis of our fractional-reserve banks entails a general financial meltdown. Rock bottom is reached, in a commodity money system, when all money substitutes have vanished and the market participants have turned to using the money commodity itself or use competing currencies, for example, other commodities or foreign paper monies. After the deflation has cleaned up the economic landscape, fractional-reserve banking and other forms of financial intermediation will play a less significant role in the economy. Firms and individuals will, at the margin, turn to financing whatever purchases they make through personal savings. In short, financial decision-making will be even more conservative and more decentralized than before.

This first scenario was very common in the nineteenth century and up to the Great Depression, which, according to Irving Fisher and the early Chicago School, was all about debt-deflation entailed by a liquidity crisis of fractional reserve banking. The scenario became less important after the introduction of deposit insurance, which for all practical purposes established 100 percent reserve banking in the U.S.[25]

---

[25]Notice that in the Great Depression deflation was not allowed to complete its work. The Fed inflated the economy after deflation had destroyed a great number of banks, reducing their total number to some 15,000—roughly the level prevailing in 1900. These select few, protected by federal deposit insurance, then surfed on the Fed-created inflation and expanded their total assets from 51.4 billion in 1933

It could have some relevance, however, in explaining the more recent financial crises in Russia, Brazil, Argentina, and certain Asian countries, in particular if the currencies of these countries at the time of the crisis could be interpreted as money substitutes for U.S. dollars.

Second, there can be intertemporal misallocations of resources when fraudulent fractional-reserve banks increase the money supply and thereby depress market interest rates below their equilibrium level. Then entrepreneurs invest too many of the available resources high up in the physical production chain, and not enough resources in the lower stages of the structure of production. The result becomes visible after some time, when a more or less great number of firms must file bankruptcy. This in turn jeopardizes their creditors, in particular fractional-reserve banks, and leads to the chain of events we described above. The difference between the second and the first scenario is in the causation of the bank run. In the former, the bank run starts more or less by accident, when one major market participant—be it out of negligence or due to unforeseeable contingencies—fails and pulls down a house of cards. By contrast, in the scenario we are now considering, the bank run is the necessary consequence of a previous misallocation of resources that resulted from a fraudulent increase of the money supply.

---

to 242.6 billion dollars in 1957. See R.W. Burgess, ed., *Historical Statistics of the United States, Colonial Times to 1957* (Washington, D.C.: Bureau of the Census, 1960).

The question is whether this scenario applied to any historical crisis is somewhat controversial. Many Austrian economists believe it fits the Great Depression and several other economic crises of the past. At any rate, it is certainly a conceivable scenario, and it also involves a heavy dose of money-substitute deflation. Hence, in this scenario too inflation ends up in a deflationary meltdown of the old ways of finance. The share of banking and financial intermediation in overall economic activity will be reduced, and financial decision-making will be even more conservative and decentralized than it is anyway.

The two foregoing scenarios both involve a more or less sudden decline of the demand for money substitutes, which entail a more or less rapid physical disappearance of these *substitutes* from circulation, as market participants switch to using base money. By contrast, in the case of paper money, it is very unlikely that there will ever be a rapid deflation in our definition—a reduction of the money supply. The reason is that paper money is protected through legal tender laws and other legislation. That leaves barter as the only legal alternative to using paper money, and barter is so much less beneficial than monetary exchange that market participants typically prefer using even very inflationary monies rather than turning to barter. In all known cases, it was only under extreme duress—when the purchasing power of their paper money holdings dwindled within hours, so that indirect exchange became impracticable—that the market participants finally ignored the laws and started using other monies than the legal tender.

The foregoing three scenarios cover probably most historical cases in which inflation has been brought to an end. If we tie this up with our comparative analysis of free and compulsory production of money and money substitutes, we come to the conclusion that deflation is not a mere redistribution game that benefits some individuals and groups at the expense of other individuals and groups. Rather, deflation appears as a great harbinger of liberty. It stops inflation and destroys the institutions that produce inflation. It abolishes the advantage that inflation-based debt finance enjoys, at the margin, over savings-based equity finance. And it therefore decentralizes financial decision-making and makes banks, firms, and individuals more prudent and self-reliant than they would have been under inflation. Most importantly, deflation eradicates the re-channeling of incomes that result from the monopoly privileges of central banks. It thus destroys the economic basis of the false elites and obliges them to become true elites rather quickly, or abdicate and make way for new entrepreneurs and other social leaders.

It is highly significant that the authors of the 1931 Macmillan Report, which analyzed the worldwide financial crisis of the time, recognized and emphasized that deflation was foremost a political problem. They clearly saw that deflation brings down the politico-economic establishment, which thrives on inflation and debts, and that it therefore brings about some circulation of the elites. The late Lord Keynes and his co-authors—among them several leaders of the London banking industry, and of the British cooperative and labor-union movements—were of course convinced that their country could not do without them.[26]

Deflation puts a brake—at the very least a temporary brake—on the further concentration and consolidation of power in the hands of the federal government and in particular in the executive branch. It dampens the growth of the welfare state, if it does not lead to its outright implosion. In short, deflation is at least potentially a great liberating force. It not only brings the inflated monetary system back to rock bottom, it brings the entire society back in touch with the real world, because it destroys the economic basis of the social engineers, spin doctors, and brain washers.[27] In light of these considerations, deflation is not merely one fundamental policy option next to the fundamental alternative of re-inflation. Rather, if our purpose is to maintain and—where necessary—to restore, a free society, then deflation is the only acceptable monetary policy.

---

[26]See "Committee on Finance and Industry Report" (London: His Majesty's Stationary Office, #3897, 1931). On the concept of circulation of elites, see Vilfredo Pareto, *Manuel d'économie politique* (Geneva: Droz, 1966), chap. 2, §§ 103–07 and chap. 7, §§ 19–21; translated as *Manual of Political Economy* (New York: Augustus M. Kelley, 1971).

[27]On the cultural implications of inflation see Paul A. Cantor, "Hyperinflation and Hyperreality: Thomas Mann in the Light of Austrian Economics," *Review of Austrian Economics* 7, no. 1 (1994).

The case of Japan might serve as a warning counter-example. The severe Japanese recession of the early 1990s was both an economic and a political threat to the establishment. In Japan, the process of consolidation and centralization of power started right after World War II, when the "economic experts" within the U.S. occupation forces imposed Keynesian and socialist policies on their former enemy. By the late 1980s, the process had advanced to such an extent that it was politically impossible to allow deflation to cleanse the economy and politics. The Japanese governments of the 1990s sought to "fix" the economic crisis through increasingly heavy doses of inflation. But the only result of this policy was to give a zombie life to the hopelessly bureaucratic and bankrupt conglomerates that control Japanese industry, banking, and politics.[28] After almost fifteen years of mindless inflation, Japan's economic crisis has turned into a fundamental political crisis that sooner or later will bring the country onto the verge of revolution.

---

[28]On the efforts of the ruling party (LDP) to bail out and prop up its allies in agriculture, banking, and construction industries, see the report of the *Economist Intelligence Unit: Country Profile Japan* (London: The Economist, 2001). For an interesting attempt to explain the current crisis in Japan as a "structural trap" rather than as a mere monetary liquidity trap, see Robert H. Dugger and Angel Ubide, "Structural Traps, Politics, and Monetary Policy" (working paper, Tudor Investment Corporation, May 2002). See also Edward Lincoln, *Arthritic Japan: The Slow Pace of Economic Reform* (Washington, D.C.: Brookings Institution, 2001). On the general issue of economic-political sclerosis see Mancur Olson, *The Rise and Decline of Nations* (New Haven, Conn.: Yale University Press, 1984).

This is also what will happen to the West, if the citizens of our countries let their governments have a free hand in monetary affairs.

VIII.

In conclusion let us restate the main points: Deflation is far from being inherently bad. Quite to the contrary, it fulfills the very important social function of cleansing the economy and the body politic from all sorts of parasites that have thrived on the previous inflation. In a word: the dangers of deflation are chimerical, but its charms are very real. There is absolutely no reason to be concerned about the economic effects of deflation—unless one equates the welfare of the nation with the welfare of its false elites. There are by contrast many reasons to be concerned about both the economic and political consequences of the only alternative to deflation, namely, re-inflation—which is of course nothing but inflation pure and simple.

The purpose of these pages is not to appeal to the reason of our monetary authorities. There is absolutely no hope that the Federal Reserve or any other fiat money producer of the world will change their policies any time soon. But it is time that the friends of liberty change their minds on the crucial issue of deflation. False thinking on this point has given our governments undue leeway, of which they have made ample and bad use. Ultimately we need to take control over the money supply out of the hands of our governments and make the production of money again subject to the principle of free association. The first step to endorsing and promoting this strategy is to realize that governments do not—indeed cannot—fulfill any positive role whatever through the control of our money.

Printed in Poland
by Amazon Fulfillment
Poland Sp. z o.o., Wrocław